Mad about...

Dinosaurs

written by Claire Hawcock
illustrated by Sue Hendra and Paul Linnet

consultant: Rupert Matthews

A catalogue record for this book is available from the British Library

Published by Ladybird Books Ltd
80 Strand London WC2R 0RL
A Penguin Company

019
© LADYBIRD BOOKS LTD MMVIII
LADYBIRD and the device of a Ladybird are trademarks of Ladybird Books Ltd

Produced by Calcium for Ladybird Books Ltd

ISBN: 9781 84646 922 0

Printed in China

Contents

Some words appear in **bold** in this book.
Turn to the glossary to learn about them.

What were dinosaurs?

Dinosaurs were **reptiles** that first walked on Earth between 203 and 225 million years ago, during a time called the **Mesozoic era**. Then suddenly, 65 million years ago, they all died out. **Fossils** of dinosaur bones show us how they may have looked.

There were many different kinds of dinosaur. Some were peaceful. Others, such as Deinonychus, were fierce hunters.

Dinosaurs were covered in thick, tough skin. However, no one knows for sure what colour they were.

6

Plant-eating Stegosaurus had two rows of bony plates that ran along its back and tail.

Apatosaurus was a giant, slow-moving plant-eater.

If you have a computer, you can download a poster of different dinosaurs from www.ladybird.com/madabout

Time of the dinosaurs

The Mesozoic era was divided into three periods: the **Triassic**, **Jurassic** and **Cretaceous**. Each period had a different **climate** and its own type of plants. Dinosaurs also changed from one period to another.

Pterosaurs

Other creatures shared the dinosaur world. Some, called pterosaurs, flew in the skies.

TRIASSIC	JURASSIC	CRETACEOUS
200–250 million years ago	145–200 million years ago	65–145 million years ago

Many leafy plants grew in the Jurassic period. That meant there was plenty of food for plant-eating dinosaurs, and they grew bigger and bigger.

Archaeopteryx was one of the earliest of birds. It had feathered wings and a feathered tail.

Brachiosaurus

Compsognathus

Stegosaurus

some creatures, such as Ichthyosaurus, swam in the seas

9

Dinosaur bodies

All dinosaurs had similar skeletons. These included a skull, spine, ribs, hips, shoulders, legs, and tail. Dinosaurs had different body shapes, depending on how they lived.

Meat-eaters' teeth were different to plant-eaters' teeth. Meat-eaters had sharp teeth for gripping and tearing flesh. Plant-eaters had flatter or rounder teeth for grinding up plants.

Diplodocus was a plant-eater

Allosaurus was a meat-eater

Large meat-eaters, like Albertosaurus, had huge skulls to carry the weight of their tooth-filled jaws.

Saltasaurus

Herrerasaurus

The first dinosaurs walked on two legs. As dinosaurs became larger, some of them walked on four legs to hold up their large stomachs.

11

Weird and wonderful

Dinosaurs came in many shapes and sizes. Some of them looked very strange!

— sail

Spinosaurus had a bony sail along its back. Blood vessels inside the sail may have warmed up in the sun. That would have kept this dinosaur warm.

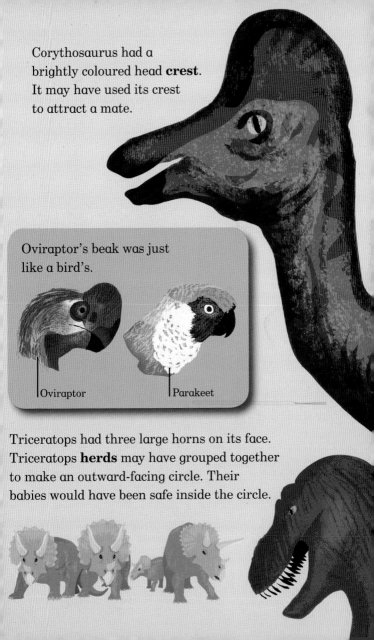

Corythosaurus had a brightly coloured head **crest**. It may have used its crest to attract a mate.

Oviraptor's beak was just like a bird's.

Oviraptor

Parakeet

Triceratops had three large horns on its face. Triceratops **herds** may have grouped together to make an outward-facing circle. Their babies would have been safe inside the circle.

Huge plant-eaters

Some of the largest dinosaurs were plant-eaters. They had to eat huge amounts of food to **survive**. The plants they ate were tough and difficult to **digest**.

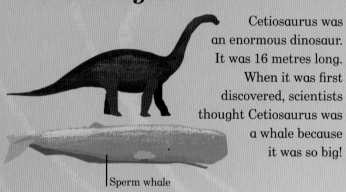

Cetiosaurus was an enormous dinosaur. It was 16 metres long. When it was first discovered, scientists thought Cetiosaurus was a whale because it was so big!

Sperm whale

Diplodocus had an extremely long back and tail. It was as long as two buses. Its four, pillar-like legs helped to keep it upright.

Triceratops' head alone was two metres long – that's the height of a fully-grown man!

Some large plant-eating dinosaurs swallowed stones to help break down the food inside their stomachs.

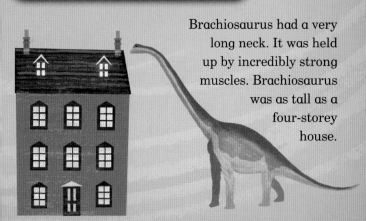

Brachiosaurus had a very long neck. It was held up by incredibly strong muscles. Brachiosaurus was as tall as a four-storey house.

15

Meat-eaters

Meat-eating dinosaurs usually had long, strong legs. They used them to run quickly, so they could catch their **prey**. They also had strong jaws, sharp teeth and deadly claws.

Allosaurus could open its jaws far apart and move them outwards to eat huge chunks of flesh.

Tyrannosaurus rex used its forward-facing eyes to see exactly how far away its prey was before it attacked.

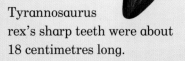

Tyrannosaurus rex's sharp teeth were about 18 centimetres long.

Velociraptor hunted in a **pack**. It was a light, fast runner that could easily catch its prey.

Deinonychus hunted in packs

swivelling toe claw

Deinonychus used its razor-sharp, swivelling toe claws to slash into the flesh of dinosaurs. By hunting in packs, Deinonychus could bring down dinosaurs much bigger than itself.

Defence

Many plant-eating dinosaurs had horns or spikes, which they used to defend themselves. Others simply used their enormous size to scare away enemies.

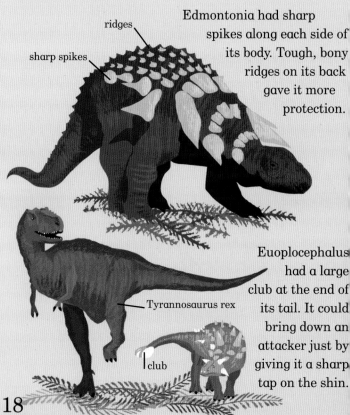

Edmontonia had sharp spikes along each side of its body. Tough, bony ridges on its back gave it more protection.

ridges

sharp spikes

Tyrannosaurus rex

Euoplocephalus had a large club at the end of its tail. It could bring down an attacker just by giving it a sharp tap on the shin.

club

18

Iguanodon jabbed its thumb spike into its attacker's throat, eyes or stomach.

thumb spike

Some dinosaurs could rear up onto their two back legs to make themselves bigger.

19

Living together

Some dinosaurs lived together.
Plant-eaters often lived in large
groups, or herds. Some meat-eaters
lived in small groups, or packs.
A few dinosaurs may have even
communicated with
each other.

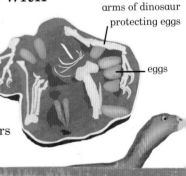

arms of dinosaur
protecting eggs

eggs

Fossilized nests show
us that baby dinosaurs
stayed in their nests
for a long time. This may
mean that mother dinosaurs
nurtured their young.

Parasaurolophus could make a trumpeting sound with its air-filled crest. The sound may have warned other dinosaurs that an enemy was near.

Hypsilophodon lived in herds.

Dinosaur hunting

Dinosaur fossils have been found all over the world. However, it is very unusual to find a complete dinosaur skeleton. Scientists who hunt for and study dinosaur fossils are called **palaeontologists** (*pay-lee-on-TOLLO-jists*).

The most commonly found fossils are bones, claws and teeth. Footprints, nests and even dung fossils are also sometimes found.

Dinosaur fossils are often found by accident. Rain and wind can wear away rock to show fossils beneath its surface. Fossils are also found when the earth cracks open, such as during an earthquake.

Palaeontologists clean up fossils and piece them together to make a dinosaur's skeleton.

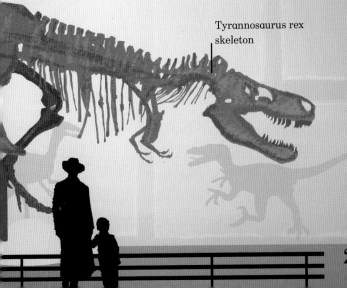

Tyrannosaurus rex skeleton

Dinosaur names

Dinosaur names are usually made up from **Latin** or Greek words. Dinosaurs are often given their names because of the way they look. For example, Tyrannosaurus means 'tyrant lizard'. Opposite is a list of all the dinosaurs in this book. It tells you how to say their names and what they mean.

Corythosaurus, the helmet lizard

Triceratops means three-horned face

Name	Say	Meaning
Albertosaurus	al-BERT-oh-SORE-us	Alberta lizard
Allosaurus	AL-oh-SORE-us	other lizard
Apatosaurus	ah-PAT-oh-SORE-us	**deceptive** lizard
Archaeopteryx	ark-ee-OPT-er-ix	ancient wing
Brachiosaurus	BRAK-ee-oh-SORE-us	arm lizard
Cetiosaurus	SEE-tee-oh-SORE-us	whale lizard
Compsognathus	KOMP-soh-NAY-thus	elegant jaw
Corythosaurus	KOH-rith-oh-SORE-us	helmet lizard
Deinonychus	die-NON-i-kus	terrible claw
Diplodocus	di-PLOH-doh-kus	double beam
Edmontonia	ed-mon-TONE-ee-ah	of Edmonton
Euoplocephalus	you-op-loh-SEF-ah-lus	well armoured head
Giganotosaurus	gig-AN-oh-toe-SORE-us	giant southern lizard
Herrerasaurus	he-REH-ra-SORE-us	Herrera's lizard
Hypsilophodon	hip-sih-LOH-foh-don	high ridge tooth
Ichthyosaurus	IK-thi-oh-SORE-us	fish lizard
Iguanodon	ig-WHA-noh-don	iguana tooth
Mamenchisaurus	MAH-men-chi-SORE-us	lizard from Mamen
Mussaurus	mus-SORE-us	mouse lizard
Oviraptor	OHV-ih-RAP-tor	egg thief
Pachycephalosaurus	PAK-ee-SEF-a-loh-SORE-us	thick-headed lizard
Parasaurolophus	par-a-SORE-oh-LOAF-us	beside Saurolophus
Pterosaur	TERR-oh-SORE	finger reptile
Saltasaurus	SALT-ah-SORE-us	of Salta
Spinosaurus	SPINE-oh-SORE-us	thorn lizard
Stegosaurus	STEG-oh-SORE-us	roof lizard
Triceratops	try-SERRA-tops	three-horned face
Troodon	TROH-oh-don	wounding tooth
Tyrannosaurus rex	tie-RAN-oh-SORE-us rex	tyrant lizard
Ultrasaurus	ULT-ra-SORE-us	ultra lizard
Velociraptor	VEL-O-si-RAP-tor	quick **plunderer**

Fantastic facts

- Dinosaur hunters look at fossilized dinosaur dung, called coprolites, to find out what dinosaurs ate.

- Some huge plant-eaters, such as Diplodocus and Brachiosaurus, may have lived for about 100 years.

- Some people think dinosaurs became **extinct** when a **meteor** hit the Earth and wiped them out.

- Many dinosaur fossils have been found in Mongolia's Gobi Desert.

- The smallest dinosaur skeleton ever found is the skeleton of a baby dinosaur called Mussaurus, or 'mouse lizard'. It can fit in the palm of a person's hand.

- 'Dinosaur' means 'terrible lizard' in Latin.

- Small, boneless creatures called ammonites died out with the dinosaurs. Lots of ammonite fossils can be found today.

- So far, about 700 different kinds of dinosaur have been found.

- Dinosaurs usually walked on their toes, just like dogs, cats and chickens. A pad of tissue on the back of the dinosaur's foot acted as a shock absorber.

- Dinosaur fossils have been found all over the world. Perhaps there are some where you live!

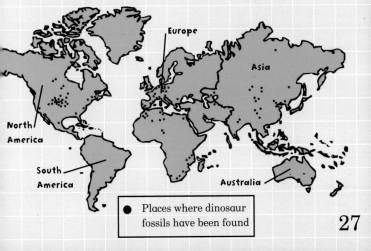

Europe

Asia

North America

South America

Australia

- Places where dinosaur fossils have been found

Amazing dinosaur awards

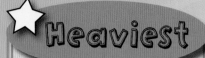

★ Heaviest

Brachiosaurus looked like a massive giraffe. It weighed between 30 and 50 tonnes – the same as ten elephants!

★ Largest

Ultrasaurus was a huge plant-eater that lived in the Jurassic Period. It was up to 39 metres long – the length of three buses!

★ Largest meat-eater

Giganotosaurus was the biggest of all meat-eating dinosaurs. It was 14.3 metres long. That's about as long as a large lorry.

Longest neck

Mamenchisaurus had the longest neck of all dinosaurs. It had 19 bones in its neck, which was 14 metres long. That's about four times longer than a giraffe's neck!

Smallest

Compsognathus was only one metre long and weighed about the same as a chicken. Although it was small, it was a fast, successful hunter.

Smartest

Troodon was probably the brightest dinosaur. For its body size, its brain was bigger than any other dinosaur. It lived in the Cretaceous period and was a fierce hunter.

Tyrannosaurus rex brain

Troodon brain

Glossary

climate – the way the weather is over a long period of time.

communicate – to 'talk' to another, usually through noise or touch.

crest – a tuft of feathers, fur or skin along the top of an animal's head.

Cretaceous – the last period of the Mesozoic era, about 65-144 million years ago.

digest – to break food down in the stomach.

deceptive – to give the wrong idea about something.

extinct – to have died out.

fossils – bones or other body parts found in the ground.

herd – a large group of plant-eating animals that live and feed together.

Jurassic – the middle period of the Mesozoic era, about 144-208 million years ago.

Latin – an old language often used by scientists to name animals and plants.

Mesozoic era – a time between 65 and 248 million years ago when dinosaurs lived on Earth.

meteor – a large rock that travels through space.

nurture – to look after.

pack – a small group of meat-eating animals of the same type.

palaeontologist – a scientist who studies the fossils of extinct animals.

plunderer – person or animal that steals from others.

prey – an animal hunted by another for food.

reptile – a cold-blooded animal whose body temperature is controlled by the temperature of the sun, air or water that surrounds it.

survive – to keep on living.

Triassic – the first period of the Mesozoic era, about 208–248 million years ago.